Forty & Wiser

REMARKABLE INSIDER SECRETS FROM WOMEN FORTY AND WISER

Jessica Peterson and Yvonne A. Jones

BYTESPRESS

PUBLISHING

CLARITY, COMMUNICATION, CONVERSION

BytesPress Publishing
Wilmington, NC

Forty and Wiser/ Jessica Peterson and Yvonne A. Jones
ISBN-10: 0-9974709-2-5
ISBN-13: 978-0-9974709-2-5

Contents

I would give all the money I have to see my grandmother one more day. She is in my heart always and I think of her daily. She was wise, practical, and feisty, but simple. Her heart was pure gold and I admire her for all that she gave and for the wisdom she held. I wish she were here today to share that wisdom.

In the meantime, until the day comes when we are together again, I dedicate this book to her.

-Jessica Peterson

Acknowledgements

First, thank you for reading this short book. At one time I called it a report, then it grew larger and I grew wiser.

Thank you, especially, to Yvonne for the wisdom and love that she gives in the world and for saying YES to delivering this book with me.

Special thanks to Candy and Angie. When Candy at writingbytes.com heard what I was up to (which was due to me asking her to be in our book) her kindness was beyond amazing when she stepped up to give advice on publishing.

Angie with www.planstoprosperwebdesign.com/ was so inspired and touched by what she heard (after having a sneak peek look at the comments) that she stepped up and provided assistance with a simple, one-page website to get this book out there in the hands of people around the globe.

And finally, thank you in advance to the wonderful women and to their friends, like you, who will share and have shared the link to grab this book in email, word of mouth, or on social media.

The gift of sharing feels so good!

Foreword

My vision for this book is to deliver powerful information that could impact or change at least one life. It was born out of events happening in my own life and the lives of women with whom I connect every day.

As I geared up to turn 40, I realized that this is a moment in life that feels very different. Women go through phases in life. I remember saying *Yahoo! I'm 21!* Then soon enough I, and all of us, experience the moment of turning 25, then 30, then 35 and then 40, and so forth. What I notice about turning 40 is that it is a moment filled with a feeling of shift. I have accomplished so much and am on edge with excitement as I look for what is coming next.

In talking to other women, I found that my reaction to this experience is not unique. My thirst to learn what is next is shared by so many other women. I realized that I kept connecting with women 40 and wiser (I like that term much better than 40 and older). It was eye-opening to discover the common theme in our conversations—they kept talking about how much inspiration they have to share and that they have a message and important information to give to the world.

Thus my vision was born. *What if I could take what little I know, ask other women in the world to share their message and combine that knowledge?* How much fun and packed with power would that be?!

I made it my goal to start my next decade in life celebrating with wisdom from many women. So the journey began and it was quick; started in April and finished in April. We, as women, strive every day to feel good, look good, have fun and find joy in life, achieve financial freedom, and so much more. My desire is for you to take the information in this book and treasure it—keep it; refer to it often, and reflect. You never know how one message can have a positive impact in your life, or someone else's, at that moment and time.

Francis Bacon said "A prudent question is one half of wisdom". These are the questions we asked:

If any woman came to you and asked for your #1 inside secret to being wiser, what would you say?

What would you say to your younger self?

If a woman wishes to connect with you, what is the best way to do so?

The answers given to our questions come from both famous and not-so-famous women. The order in which their responses appear in this book is random, no weight is given to any answer over another. Yvonne and I asked the questions of women who come from all backgrounds; we all have wisdom to share.

Jessica Peterson

ONE

LORI HART

ꟿ y number one secret to being wiser is staying open to learning and growing from the mentors I admire as well as continuing to learn about my profession so that I am on top of what is current.

Be open to learning outside your comfort zone even if you choose to delegate it later.

I say to my younger self—you can do it.

Do what you love.

Stay the course.

Learn everything and put it into action.

Acknowledge your accomplishments.

Stay in love and gratitude.

Get out of your own way.

Love yourself first, even things you don't like about yourself.

Forgive yourself. These lessons help you grow.

If a woman wishes to connect with me, this way is best:
lorihart@lorihart.com

TWO

SILVANIA FERRARI

D o not say everything you know.

Do not do all you can.

Do not believe in everything you hear.

Do not spend all you have.

To the young I say:

Love thy father and thy mother and everything will go well.

If a woman wishes to connect with me, this way is best —
https://www.facebook.com/silvania.ferrari.96 .

THREE

MARY BORSE

T here really is no secret that I know of. I think you learn from your mistakes, receive your experience, embrace it, hold on tight, get through it with faith. You can't fight it or hide it.

Be your best authentic self you can be. Do not compare yourself to others. They may have already learned lessons from other events in their life. You are unique and only you are in the stage of life learning you are in.

Receive your gifts, and share them. If you don't think you have gifts, look deeper.

Get out of your own way, and push through your fears. Open yourself up to receiving more abundance and blessings, experience gratitude. Learn how to open up to more money, abundance, and lessons. Figure out how you are blocking yourself from receiving abundance.

Unlock your mind and open up to positive energy flow. Move more and listen more. Be more conscious, more aware.

Learn to be kind to yourself. Take responsibility for your own actions, design your own life, and own it!

P.S. There are no shortcuts!

If a woman wishes to connect with me, this way is best — https://www.facebook.com/Mary.Borse

FOUR

KRISTIE KNIGHT

J ust be. It is that simple. Be real. Be raw. Just be.

Often women are taught to live in the shadow of others. It can be parents, siblings, employers, spouse, you name it. It is in these shadows that loss of the sense of self occurs.

The sense of self is essential to each and every moment of our lives. It is the guiding force in each decision we make. With a strong and solid sense of self, a woman is confident. In confidence comes obtainment of the dreams and goals aspired.

Just be is the essence of soulful self. It is the ability to sit in your own heart space, drop to your metaphoric knees, and love. It is the ability to love without borders.

9

Love is not to be used as a weapon or with discrimination. It is to be given freely, without reservation. That is often a challenge when the sense of self is unfounded, lost, or squelched by life. Please note, if your sense of self is unfounded, lost, or squelched, it has been permitted. You have permitted it. Do you understand how powerful that truth is?

When you recognize your ability to grant permission to be forgotten, you gain the insight of the permission to be remembered again. Yes, only you can make it happen. How? I know, it feels overwhelming. Many times clients come to my office searching for their purpose. They do not understand their lives and why there is so much misfortune or lack of joy. It is in the darkest hour I whisper, be real.

The ability to be real indicates strength and confidence. Many fear simmering in their own realness. What do you fear when you are quiet and allow the realness to surface? It is an awe-inspiring presence that has an immense amount of opportunity and power. Fear, fear, stifles the ability to be real.

To be real is to own who you are and what you bring to the table. It is not about showcasing your weaknesses, or intently compensating for our weaknesses. It is the amazing ability to recognize and elevate your strengths.

To be real requires acceptance of the soulful self. When you are real, other's flock to you. It is a level of energy and magnetism that is wanted by all. In fact, many believe it is infectious, or contagious, and will long to be in your presence. What do I mean? Well, you know, when you walk into a room full of strangers and that one woman stands out. You think to yourself, 'I want to be her friend.' She has it. She owns the realness of her soulful self.

How does a woman gain the love and acceptance of her soulful self? I am so glad you asked! Be raw. What does it mean to be raw? In all rawness, you lie soulfully naked to the world; to each and every person you encounter. It is in your rawness of your soulful self that others grow. Yes! Did you read that? Other's grow in your rawness. I like to use the word vulnerability as well. I know what you're thinking, 'But I can't.' What stirs that feeling? Oh yes, fear.

Fear of rejection and abandonment. Well guess what Sista, if you are real and raw, in the state of just be, and then are rejected, that person is not part of your purpose! Their path is of another. Instead of feeling at loss, embrace the perceived rejection as an opportunity to deepen your self-awareness and the type of women you desire to be surrounded by. The only ones I prefer are those who can walk along side, loving unconditionally, and living in the state of real, raw, and being their soulful self!

What would I say to my younger self?

Dearest Kristie, My Love;

Yes, yes, it has been a dreadful road at times. You have endured much that life has spilled out. But you see, you made each choice that led to that moment. As much as I desire to spare you of the pain you have encountered, I want you to embrace it. Embrace each moment as you experience it. Know that it is the culmination of each moment that has created the amazing woman you will become.

Remember, grace. Grace is essential to the development of your soulful self. Yes, you are going to make mistakes, betray others, feel as if you are so very alone; have grace. Know that the sun will still set. With every sun that sets, it will rise. It will rise just as you will. It is in the rise you will transform lives.

Be true to yourself. Love and serve others. Give freely despite the intense rejection and doubt from the world. The world can be a cruel place, but know that if you see cruelty, change the channel. It is in you the filter exists. Yes, you have the strength and empowerment to change the channel and rise.

Each day Kristie, as you age, live your life in service to others. Abundance will come your way as you share abundantly. No Kristie, abundance is not determined by the brand of shoes you wear, the vehicle you own, or the house you live in. It is defined by the number of lives you will touch. It is defined by the level of realness and rawness you have lived in service to others.

Kristie, in all things you do, be real, be raw, just be.

If a woman wishes to connect with me, this way is best — kristie@kristieknights.com

FIVE

VICKY FLINT

To being wiser:
  Trust your gut.
  To my younger self:
  Your life matters, you are soooo valuable and loved.

  If a woman wishes to connect with me, this way is best —
  https://www.facebook.com/vicky.flint

SIX

KAREN FINOCCHIO

The number one insider secret to being wiser, is to stay young and learn something new every day. Don't be afraid to attempt something completely out of your comfort zone.

Surround yourself with people who have a different career path than yours and learn from them. I love hanging out with the 20 and 30 years olds in my office. They have a fresh perspective, are open minded, and are willing to teach me. I am learning bits of code right now. WHY? Because they'll teach me and they think it's awesome that I want to learn. Failure is proof you are trying. Boom! If you are not failing at learning something, you are not trying hard enough and taking risks. Step out of your comfort zone. Failure is an incident, NOT a tattoo.

If a woman wishes to connect with me, this way is best —
www.onetoughmuther.net/

SEVEN

KATIE DREW JENSEN

Truly go inward and trust your inner voice. It's there if you tap into it. Embrace the challenges you face as much as the success. We learn from the struggles. There would be no success without hardship.

Find an older mentor and listen deeply to their truths. Age brings wisdom!

Don't sweat the small things and pick your battles wisely. Raising children mainly as a single parent, I look back and see how I tried to make everything perfect, making everyone crazy. Let go of the unimportant things. Concentrate on the beauty or you may miss it. Be way kinder to yourself

If a woman wishes to connect with me, this way is best —
http://katiedrewcoaching.com/

EIGHT

MICHELLE HOGLAN

f any woman came to me and asked for my number one secret to being wiser, I would say don't take yourself too seriously.

#LifeHappens!!

What would I say to my younger self?

Keep looking towards the future but don't forget to take the time to enjoy the present.

Live now, it goes by so quickly!

If a woman wishes to connect with me, this way is best —
https://www.facebook.com/michelle.hoglan

NINE

BARB FINDLAY

You are responsible for your life and what you want. No one is responsible for your happiness and success. Being Wise means having the power of discerning and judging properly as to what is true or right.

What most women don't realize is that we have the power, and yet we give it away and become small.

Live life with integrity and by your values and know your truth, then you are never second guessing yourself. It is when we allow another's opinion to influence our decision making that we start giving our power away.

Listen to your heart, and your elders and people you respect. Most of the time older people (parents, grandparents, teachers, and pastors) are wiser because they have lived life through a different set of times; through their eyes they see things that we cannot, as we are too close. They give us the perspective that we are too close to see.

Trust your gut instinct. When the inner self tells you or sends you a warning, pay attention. It is your conscious, early warning signal. Listen and pay attention.

Get your education!! Don't wait. You will pay for your education one way or the other, either through higher education, or through life experience.

Learn grace and respect. Show others grace, as you are only seeing what the person wants you to see, you don't know their whole story. Treat everyone with respect, starting with yourself. People are always watching and you never know when you are being a role model.

Don't compare yourself to anyone else, God made you as a unique individual, with a set of talents no one else has. Be who you are supposed to be, as you are awesome.

Smile!!! When you smile the world smiles with you!!

If a woman wishes to connect with me, this way is best —
https://www.facebook.com/barb.findlay

TEN

HEIDI MARKUS

Number one secret to being wiser is to listen to your own intuition; you really do know the answer for what is best for you.

And to my younger self, I would tell you that so much of what you worry about today is never going to happen, so enjoy life more and don't be afraid to take risks.

If a woman wishes to connect with me, this way is best —
https://www.facebook.com/heidimarkus

ELEVEN

BRANDY BROOKS

Despite my imperfections, I accept who I am, while striving to be the best version of myself. The love from those around me coupled with my belief gives me things the mirror can never reflect.

Every one of us is an inspiration in some way, so set a good example and be proud to be the true you.

Love yourself first and you'll become irresistibly loveable to anyone who's worth your concern

If a woman wishes to connect with me, this way is best —
http://www.soleful.com

TWELVE

TERESIA ROSE REED

The thing I have thought of many times over the years, is how important it is to keep your promises to yourself. We make promises to ourselves everyday based on what is said by that still, small voice inside us that guides us.

Trusting yourself and whatever that still voice is saying is truly important.

This is true of those promises you make to yourself about how you allow others to treat you and about what you are willing to do or not in your personal and professional life.

If you make a decision that you will not sell yourself short, or allow people into your life who are not healthy for you, then do that—keep the promise.

It has played out more than once that when I choose to ignore those promises about the depth and quality of the life I chose to live and with whom, it was very costly, both from the heart and from a financial point of view.

I think we are born with certain internal indicators about what and who is good for us. We just need to honor and trust those little red flags when they go off.

If a woman wishes to connect with me, this way is best —
https://www.facebook.com/teresia.reed

THIRTEEN

ROXIE ELLIS

ike Kenny Rogers once said, "Know when to hold'em and know when to fold'em." I am true believer that there comes a time to let go. You have to be willing to change with the times.

To my younger self I say, trust in Jesus more, I know I would of had less stress.

If a woman wishes to connect with me, this way is best —
https://www.facebook.com/roxienormanellis

FOURTEEN

KELLY ROBBINS

Have learned to trust myself, particularly my intuition. Rather than making fast decisions and then changing my mind when someone looks at me wrong I pause, listen to my body, and then act. I have drastically reduced second-guessing myself with this method. I have also stopped wondering what 'the right thing' to do is and started focusing on the right thing to do for Kelly. Major wise move and serious game changer!

To my younger self: I love you. Everything will turn out exactly perfect. Stop doing what you think you should do and figure out who you are and what you want. NOW. It's important.

If a woman wishes to connect with me, this way is best —
kelly@kellyrobbins.net

FIFTEEN

KELLY FROST

f a woman came to me and asked me for my number one inside secret to being wiser, I would tell her that there is no secret.

Wisdom comes from experience.

Wisdom comes from being open to experiences and taking in all that life has to offer.

Wisdom comes from listening more, and sometimes talking less. Every day we are given opportunities to learn from our experiences; even negative experiences teach us life lessons. They may be the hardest lessons to learn, but often they are the best lessons, and the ones that help us to grow.

Wisdom comes from being hurt, healing, and becoming stronger because of it.

Wisdom comes from making mistakes, learning from them, and knowing how to avoid them.

Wisdom comes from getting knocked down, brushing yourself off, and learning how to get back up again!

There is no secret to being wiser, wisdom comes from your own life experiences and every one gains their own wisdom at their own time.

However, time is a precious commodity; take every opportunity you have and be open to experiences, especially if they are out of your comfort zone—that's where the good stuff is!

Never stop learning. Invest in yourself! Every day is an opportunity to learn something new. Become as valuable as you can, and don't forget to value yourself!

Have confidence and be courageous, say yes to as many experiences and opportunities as you can, even if they terrify you! The accomplishment will feel 100 times more amazing than the terror!

Proximity is power, surround yourself with others who are as driven as you are to succeed and still be ethical, charitable, and kind. These are your people; this is your tribe! Together you will do great things in the world. You will lift each other up, you will help others, you will give back, you will make a positive difference in this world.

Continue on your path in life, I am proud of you!

If a woman wishes to connect with me, this way is best — www.frostexecutiveservices.com/

SIXTEEN

DAWN MARIE WESTMORELAND

I t took landing in the Mental Health ward after two years of horrific bullying for being a government *whistleblower* before I took complete charge of my life. I looked in the metal mirror after three days of being in the ward and made up my mind to never feel like a *victim* again in my life.

This began the process of completely changing my entire life and taking 100% accountability for my belief system. It also motivated me to speak around workplace bullying, write a book, become a professional coach, and use my HR skills to help others who face workplace bullying and discrimination.

If a woman came to me and wanted me to share some of my empowerment tips, I would say to her that *sometimes our gifts in life come in ugly wrapping paper.*

When we are not living our soul's purpose, we may get pushed to be uncomfortable about moving out of a relationship, a job, or any situation, and become aligned with our purpose on this earth. We are not being punished—we are being pushed to use our skill sets and creativity in the right job for ourselves. That may be working for another company or becoming an entrepreneur.

I would tell my younger self that life does not have *challenges*, but opportunities to grow and become the best version of ourselves.

Every experience in life can be a lesson to learn how to love and respect ourselves more. We can learn how to overcome our hardships, set healthy boundaries in our lives, and own our old stories, instead of our old stories owning us.

If you notice that negative patterns are repeating themselves, over and over—you have not conquered the lesson. When you are following your soul's purpose—the right people and resources will appear

If a woman wishes to connect with me, this way is best —
www.TheEmpoweredWhistleblower.com
https://www.facebook.com/dawn.marie.westmoreland

SEVENTEEN

EDITH SIEGA LEE

ife is full of dualisms: comfort and hardship, courage and fear, love and hate, success and failure, wealth and deprivation, brightness and darkness, youth and old age, fulfillment and bereavement, day and night, sunrise and sunset, so on and so forth.

In my seventy-four years, I've experienced these dualities starting from birth during World War 2, growing up in poverty, going to college as a naive barrio girl, teaching for ten years in a very poor institution with very meager pay, leaving my country to marry someone I had not even met, widowhood, remarriage, breast cancer, loss of job and loss of home, so on and so forth.

However, with my strong belief in God, I chose to dwell on the positive side of these dualisms and came out triumphant. It was the love of family, friends and everyone I was blessed to meet that made me who I am now and it was in the challenge that I became strong. Every experience was used as a springboard to my success and made me wise as I face the next day. At the end of day as I reflect through my life, I smile with an imaginary tap on my shoulder and quietly compliment myself for the wisdom and good judgement I developed, "Wow, I really did that, thank you Lord!"

I would tell my younger self to value every moment and not to waste any time dwelling on the foolish and unimportant things in life. Make use of my youth in dreaming dreams, making goals and work to the utmost to realize those dreams and goals for the betterment of self, family, and society as a whole.

If a woman wishes to connect with me, this way is best —
https://www.facebook.com/edithsiegalee/about

EIGHTEEN

VICKI CONLEY

intentionally hang around and learn from smarter people and take quiet time to process this crazy world. I didn't always do that, now I find it's a must. To my younger self I say that you are great at making friends and recognizing the quality in and of relationships. Keep doing what you're doing.

Find a way to make money doing what you love. It's true—you will never work a day in your life when that happens. You have to believe that you can, envision it, see it. Keep taking action toward those crazy ideas, make them happen and figure out how to juggle it all. You never know what I'll be up to!

If a woman wishes to connect with me, this way is best —
http://www.Laptoplyfe.com

NINETEEN

DR. ELSIE CROWNINSHIELD

My number one secret to be wiser is to listen before you talk and think before you react to others in all situations.

I would tell my younger self not to make decisions quickly or based on emotions and learn to apply emotional intelligence in all situations. The choices we make early on in life in our personal and professional lives will affect us for the rest of our life, so take the time to think every situation through very carefully, choose wisely.

Take as much time as you need to seek the appropriate advice and counseling as necessary.

If a woman wishes to connect with me, this way is best —
elsiednp@gmail.com

41

TWENTY

VAL BULLERMAN

f any woman came to me and asked for my number one inside secret to being wiser I would say, listen more than you speak. Make connections and learn life-long habits.

When you are able to make these actions a daily practice, you will grow and expand quickly. Never assume you know the answer—always look for the lesson, even in an unfortunate situation. Lead with love. Love yourself and others more, do what you love, make decisions based on love, not fear.

If a woman wishes to connect with me, this way is best —
https://www.facebook.com/vbullerman/about

TWENTY-ONE

TONJA WARING

Knowledge comes from books. Wisdom comes from experience. Choose to experience all life has to offer. Play with the possibilities and have fun. Know that any mistakes or failures are a great thing, because there are no mistakes or failures. Every experience we have, to our liking or not, develops wisdom and is a stone on the path to being a wise woman.

Assume that EVERYTHING (And, I mean everything.) is for your highest and best. As you go through life and look back, you realize you wouldn't change a thing and that it really was for the best; even if it was a bitter pill to swallow in the moment.

Also, listen intently; especially to children. Children are gurus in small bodies. Their minds are the closest to God's mind, and they deliver fundamental truths. They are always wanting to show us the simple way to live life in a fun and joyful way. They are the best at experiencing life. Let them show you how.

Spend five minutes a day looking in the mirror and send loving and kind thoughts to yourself. Do you see your eyes? Do you see how beautiful they are? God created your eyes just for you.

Look. Do you see your heart? Do you know the goodness that resides within you? You are a beautiful creation. There is no one like you. No one who looks like you. No one who thinks like you.

Spend the time to really get to see yourself and to know yourself. You are beautiful beyond measure. If you can't see yourself for who you are, if you can't love and appreciate the miraculous being that you are, how do you expect anyone else to see you?

If a woman wishes to connect with me, this way is best —
www.TonjaWaring.com

TWENTY-TWO

JANIECE RENDEN

The secret to being wiser is to believe in yourself. No matter where you are in the cycle of life, you have something to offer and share. We have an obligation to help others who are searching for more.

Gary Barnes, a great mentor of mine said, "We are all on the same journey in life the only difference is we are all at different mile markers."

Being wiser is knowing you have something within that will never let you down. Your seed of greatness is meant to blossom and you are the only one who can nourish it to fruition. Along the journey in life, we meet people who will give us fertilizer to grow our seed of greatness. There are also people along our journey who are the weeds in our garden. They will suck up our energy and deplete our soil and our seed of greatness will die.

47

Know your worth; know the difference between fertilizer and weeds. Understand your greatness; believe in "You". Find the fertilizer to grow your gifts. Enjoy the journey and become fertilizer for others.

What would I say to my younger self? Oh my beautiful child, you have an amazing future ahead. I know you do not have the ability to see all the amazing lives you will touch by your story, but trust in You. Keep putting one foot in front of the other to follow your passion, go forward and dream.

Yes, you are going to have setbacks and trials in life. What you think you want—the guy, the job, the ideal life—might not happen. Do not let setbacks derail your belief in yourself. Believe and know there is so much more out there. Continue on your journey, gather up all the mistakes, regrets, and disappointments and realize they are life lessons to connect with others. Your vision is not mature enough to see and focus in on the big picture. Trust and believe your path will unfold and the vision will become absolutely clear and amazing.

God has a path for you. His plan is bigger and better than what you can imagine. He will guide you along your journey if you let Him. Trust the curves in life and know the curves are temporary. The curves are there to make you stronger and appreciate the smooth road in life. Let the curves guide you to the open road of dreams, passion, and joy.

If a woman wishes to connect with me, this way is best —
https://www.facebook.com/janiece.rendon

TWENTY-THREE

HEATHER WATKINS

'd say that the secret to being wiser is learning to see myself in a more comprehensive light beyond the lens of limitations.

As a woman born with Muscular Dystrophy and a cane-user for the past 10 years, I can affirm disability has informed and evolved my perspective. It has factored into so much of my decision-making involving housing, education, work, socializing, shopping, parenting, and more.

I'm grateful that my biology has contributed to my biography in meaningful ways I'd never dreamed. Seeing ourselves in our wholeness puts the details in context and rounds out the richness of being.

I would tell my younger self to aim for being authentic, which is a revolutionary act in itself, and to connect with women of all abilities especially women with disabilities. It is in commonality that we often find community.

Connect with women who have a range of experience who can help empower and illuminate aspects of your personal journey that don't often see the light.

Never doubt that your voice has value and your perspective has worth. I am always excited about meeting more sisters who challenge antiquated beliefs I may be harboring and implore me to vibe higher. That brilliance is motivating and fuels the spirit!

If a woman wishes to connect with me, this way is best —
https://www.facebook.com/hwatkins

DEANNA ROBINSON

My secret to being wiser, is to be still and listen to your still, small voice. Slow down. You know, it's not what someone else is doing that matters, or what they are wearing, or whom they are hanging out with. Be true to yourself, and do what has significance for you. Your life matters. You only breathe for you. You have something that no one else has: being you. Offer yourself to the world. You being you betters the world around you.

I would tell my younger self that you get to decide your life. Consciously make decisions instead of allowing circumstances to dictate how you show up. Be deliberate. Do it now, no waiting for a circumstance to be different than what it is. Be the person that is BLESSED! Show up as blessed. You've got this!

If a woman wishes to connect with me, this way is best —
deanna@dentistryitspersonal.com

TWENTY-FIVE

JUDY BRAHAM

N ever be too proud to listen—really listen—to the advice of those who are older, more educated, or more experienced than you.

When I was younger, I thought, like so many of us, that I already knew it all. I didn't need anyone else to tell me how to live my life. I wasn't going to make the same dumb mistakes that everyone else made. I was too smart for that!

Naturally, I made those same dumb mistakes, and plenty of new ones too!

I learned as I became older and wiser that successful people PAY advisors and mentors for their advice for a reason! I could tap into that wisdom by simply learning to ask—and LISTEN to—the advice of those in my life who were older, successful, and more experienced—all without spending a cent!

Take better care of your body. Again, I didn't listen to all that GOOD advice about eating right, exercising, and following a good skin care routine. I am now only 54 years old and I already have osteoporosis and wrinkles. Yikes! Not to mention my body feels like I'm 84 years old.

Don't have the mindset that you're indestructible or that illness only happens to other people.

Take good care of what God blessed you with—it's all you will have while here on this Earth.

If a woman wishes to connect with me, this way is best — judyb0711@outlook.com

TWENTY-SIX

PAMELA MCKAY-STUCKERT

on't sell yourself short, you've worked hard to be the woman you are today. Expect those around you to treat you with respect, kindness, and love.

I would say to my younger self, learn as much as possible, see all there is to see, and do what you love. Do it all while being positive.

Also, be your own best friend. Be a person you'd like to hang out with.

If a woman wishes to connect with me, this way is best —
prpam.mango@gmail.com

TWENTY-SEVEN

DR. TAFFY WAGNER

Approval starts within you and not without. If you have to look to others for approval or accolades, those same people will tear you down. Don't give people that authority.

A support system doesn't have to be big. It only requires a couple of people who will protect your character not your feelings, tell you when you are right or wrong. People who always say yes don't have your best interest at heart.

Be comfortable with who you are, your gifts and talents. Do not try to conform to who everyone else think you should be. You will find peace and happiness within your true self instead of a made up one.

If a woman wishes to connect with me, this way is best —
ericandtaffy@ownyourhealthcare.com

TWENTY-EIGHT

JESSICA PETERSON

The number one piece of wisdom I can share is difficult to select. There is so much I want to give and share. Now I understand what a struggle it must have been for the other women featured in this book to select only one piece of wisdom.

I have to say it is to live life fully while keeping things simple. You might think that is an oxy-moron, but it is not. We all have dreams, so dream big!

Do not limit yourself. Stop being stuck and making things complicated. Perfectionism gets in the way and creates complications. Get out there and make it happen with a rock solid plan from the experts while being selective about whom you are with during it all.

It is OK to change your journey and dreams. Being stuck is a bad place to be. A friend of mine, Mechelle Beddoe Dittmer, shared words of wisdom from her mother.

She said, "Life is like a bus. We are all in charge of our own bus; we are drivers of our own bus. People will get on our bus at the right time and get off at the right time."

It is OK when someone gets off. It's time to allow them to get off! It allows room for more people. Be selective about whom you allow.

Create quality relationships along the journey. In the end, the right people will be there with you. And remember to smile, be positive, and laugh along the way.

What I envision is looking at my younger self, smiling and hugging her. I would start out by saying everything may not seem ok right now but trust me it will be. You are loved and know that you are on to great things in this world that will light you up and create happiness.

If a woman wishes to connect with me, this way is best —
https://www.facebook.com/jessicacustomerwowproject

OLA LOMBARDI

I f a woman came to me and asked for the number one inside secret to being wiser, I would tell her to travel in her 20s or even earlier. Get to know different cultures and meet people.

Continue your education, be open minded, and explore.

Take risks. Do not be afraid to make mistakes because that is how you learn.

Follow your heart but be reasonable. Hangout out with positive people and don't let others to put you down and make you feel that you are not good enough.

Be a giver and humble, with balance to avoid people taking advantage of you.

Be bold, be a fighter, and take charge.

I would say to my younger self that I enjoyed my childhood, teenage years, 20s. I don't regret anything.

My wish is I had taken classes in painting or other artistic venues sooner. All my life I thought I had no talent. When I was a child someone told me that I had no talent. Unfortunately, that statement remained in my mind.

The good news is I took up painting and discovered that I like it.

Do not listen to any negativity in your life.

If a woman wishes to connect with me, this way is best — ola@olalombardi.com

THIRTY

SHAHARA WRIGHT MENCHAN

Proverbs 9:10 says "The fear of the Lord is the beginning of wisdom: and the knowledge of the holy is understanding." I am wise because I have constantly worked to develop my relationship with God.

When I turned forty, I was in a dark place. For the previous two years, I had been going through some difficult financial issues. I was in a fog and really could not hear God speak to me. I remember my mom threw a party for me and I was so touched by her gesture that I was determined to move past my negative place.

It was then I decided to go back to what I already knew but had somehow forgotten. My situation was not man-made and my solution would not be man-made. God is the author of all and but for Him, I would be lost.

I changed my prayers and began to ask Him to show me what He wanted me to do. I wish I could say that everything from that point was perfect. It was not and is not. I went through a divorce and business break-up last year. Despite that, I am still clear about one thing: God is with me and whatever direction he tells me to take, I will.

My younger self, made both terrible decisions and really great decisions. There were many choices that lead to great joy and great sorrow. The only thing I would tell my younger self it to continue to seek after God in all that you do. But I already knew that when I was younger, I just did not always follow my own awesome advice!

If a woman wishes to connect with me, this way is best —
Swright@theceoeffect.net

THIRTY-ONE

LISA RAYMOND

wrote a poem in my freshman English course titled, *I Am.* I wrote it because I felt lost inside. I was alone, had few friends, and was struggling with being away from home. The truth is, I felt different. I was the alien in the room.

The first line is, *I am the color of creamed caramel coffee...*

At that time, the visual worked because I struggled with my skin tone, and the 'creamed caramel coffee' reference allowed me to identify with self. The rest of the poem was a reflection of all the things that I wasn't. Thinking of it now, it was an attempt at empowerment that made me feel more depressed and alone at that particular moment in my life.

I rewrote the poem some years later, and it's become my personal anthem. It is a challenge to self to remain my own cheerleader when everyone else falls away. It has become a continual affirmation not of what I could have been, or might be. It is my here, now, and future. So these are my words for being wiser, to any person and to my younger self.

I AM

I AM the color of creamed caramel coffee. I AM tall, warm, and beautiful. I AM not what you expected me to be, I AM one who moves mountains. I AM a survivor of illness, racism, and hate. I AM tough!

I AM innovative, passionate, and constantly moving forward. I AM always thinking of what's next.

I AM too busy being successful to reflect on what I'm not. I AM seeing all that I AM.

I AM smart, I AM present, I AM ethical but most of all, I AM PHENOMINAL!

At the end of the day, I AM still learning and growing, and guess what...so are YOU.

What you say, you do become. Stay positive and continually affirm all that YOU ARE! Begin each day with positive "I AM's", write it in a journal, on the wall, wherever your eyes can see it.

Become your own best friend and cheerleader! To change your life, you have to change your attitude and how you see yourself.

Ethically speak to yourself with love and kindness every day. EVERY DAY!

If a woman wishes to connect with me, this way is best —
https://www.facebook.com/LisaRaymondNow

THIRTY-TWO

NICOLE MONTEZ

100% Learning! Learn every chance you get. Read books, blogs and inspiration as much as you can, listen to speakers, talks, podcasts and success stories.

Learn by reflection on choices you've made, good and bad, and what you would do differently. Have meaningful conversations and don't be afraid to ask difficult questions and learn from those ahead of you.

Be brave! Don't hold back, you'll never regret giving it everything you have. It's ok to shine as bright as you can. Leave it all on the table.

If a woman wishes to connect with me, this way is best —
https://www.facebook.com/nicolekmontez

THIRTY-THREE

TARRA FLORES SLOAN

One amazing victory in life that took me years to achieve and that I live by is to provide space to be silent. Daily, I give myself space to ask questions and prepare myself to hear the answers. By sitting in silence even for 10 minutes a day, I'm able to hear with confidence my inner voice and what truly I need to hear in response.

Sounds simple enough, right? Hmm…. Most often, I vibrate knee jerk thoughts. And whilst bashing about in my normal state I would usually not provide my intuition with enough fuel to catapult myself into my next bold move.

Sitting still for 30 seconds is difficult for me. In the shower for 10 minutes (okay more like 15), my thoughts are parading around with flags and explosions. I make a list that can go something like this:

Get groceries,

Enroll in today's yoga class by phone,

Edit Chapter 3 Empowerment webinar

What I am doing to my mind is to keep it occupied in-stead of freeing my mind and allowing myself to connect to my world and create a vaster space with which to expand, explore, and execute my plans.

My new shower routine includes my affirmations and a better plan of using my time wisely. Before showering, I sit in silence and meditate for 10-30 minutes. After, I stay still and use my inner voice to ask questions and listen for the answers. My spirit is renewed and breathing life into me.

Then it all goes away and my physical body leaps up to shower and rush through my day, working all day and into the night on my passions because I also feel very alive doing this. Which is okay.

It is challenging to sit still. That's why you should start with just a couple full and complete minutes, and graduate on to adding more minutes. Even now as I sit here at the computer, there was a glitch and while waiting for it to reboot or whatever you call it, I could not simply be still and think. Instead I grabbed my coffee, pressed keys on my keyboard with a jolt, put a colita in my hair (ponytail), and checked my emails from my phone. Finally, I was able to get into my computer pro-gram.

This is sitting, but it is not what I mean by creating space in silence with intentions. By sitting still and providing space, I mean to sit with the intention to close my eyes and meditate, then to ask the questions I want to ask, then to listen for an-swers. I sort of re-boot my mind, so to speak, clearing it up, creating disk space, and when I return to my work I am feeling free, energetic, and most often on fire. I get more done in less time; I make decisions with lightning speed. Battles are picked more easily.

You may not know this, but what you really want for your daily life is to feel good, all the time, to be free and feel at peace. I want all of this, and also a billion dollars wouldn't be so bad either. (Wink)

To my younger self, I would say. Tarra? Wow! You have no idea how powerful you are. Come here and let me hold you. Wrapping my arms around you I want you to really hear me when I say, this is all temporary.

When someone hurts you, you don't have to take it and be strong. You can cry, and feel, and love yourself.

You definitely are pretty.

You definitely are super smart.

You definitely are headed for a successful life.

You don't have to see the whole list, just write your goals out and do the first item. Then the next.

Mentors are headed your way; they will be empowered women. Believe them. Listen to them. Follow them.

Ignore the haters; their journey is a hard one. Don't get mixed up in that, it leads nowhere.

If you really want your life to be different, it's okay to choose better for yourself, to protect yourself—even from people who are in charge of your child-self. You are allowed to refuse them the right to take advantage of you—to abuse you.

You do have fight in you, use that. You are not responsible for the safety and welfare of others, or of their feelings; this includes your family.

You are introverted, but this is okay. You still are funny and fun to be around, and people enjoy your company.

You don't have to be a soldier and put walls around yourself, with big hair, black plastic bracelets, black eyeliner, black lipstick, derby with old English letters, white creased t-shirts, black Dickey's and china flats.

You don't have to be "hard". You don't have to merely survive life. You can enjoy it, fully.

Find people who are kind and good to you, hang on to them and return the love. The things that may seem boring to others, that are passions for you, are your gifts.

You are capable of anything you want to do and you will prove this as time goes on. Never settle for second best, it is not giving to do this, it is not selfless to do this.

You deserve the best always, and by living in this space, you will create an example for your children to follow, and for the people who you will end up mentoring to follow as well.

Your world is about you connecting to others of like mind and spirit. No one will be exactly like you, think like you, make decisions like you, look like you. You do not have to fit in with what is the "now".

If you want blonde hair, then do it. If you want to move out of state, do it. If you want to write a book and your boyfriend tells you that you don't have enough life experience, do it anyway. Maybe, just may-be, it will make Number One Best Seller. Just manifest it all—because why not you? And make your next bold move. Always.

If a woman wishes to connect with me, this way is best —
https://www.facebook.com/tarrafloressloan

THIRTY-FOUR

VIVEKA VON ROSEN

o What Only You Can Do. The number one thing I would tell my younger self, and any woman starting out or wanting to improve her business is, Invest in Yourself. Don't invest in Get Rich Quick schemes. Truly invest in YOU.

You might want to join a mastermind or support group. Or find a good affordable graphics person to help you create an excellent logo and visual brand for yourself. Or pay for some education in areas of your business that need strengthening (like social media marketing or content creation).

But most importantly, don't try to do everything yourself. One of the best pieces of advice I ever received (and I wish I'd heeded it sooner and more often) is, do what only you can do!

Hire a VA or assistant to help do the stuff that is eating away at your time and mental capacity. Just because you are a solopreneur or small business owner, does not mean you have to do it all yourself!

When I hired my first assistant, I was able to cover her salary the first month! With my mind and time free of menial and mind-numbing labor, I could focus on what I did best: content creation, serving my clients, and getting new clients. I don't think it's a coincidence that shortly after hiring Crystal, I got a book deal with Wiley, because I had all that free time to write. My editor saw and liked what I was writing about and called me about the book.

I also would NEVER have been able to write the book without Crystal and then Nicole helping me to run my business!

You are not alone. It took me almost 10 years to finally invest in my business by getting a really good CRM and email automation program (Infusionsoft) and hiring the right people to help me with it. I sure wish I had done that earlier too, because I made enough in my first launch to pay for the Infusionsoft program and the people who help me run it for a whole year, with money left over! Everything else we do this year is gravy.

So even if you think you can't afford it, stop drinking Starbucks and buying shoes for a month and save your money to hire an assistant. See just how much more productive and successful you can be!

If a woman wishes to connect with me, this way is best —
http://linkedintobusiness.com/

THIRTY-FIVE

KAREN DEIS

P ractice assertiveness! It's different than being aggressive. Assertiveness is having confidence in yourself, your thoughts, and your actions. It takes practice. It takes educating yourself. It takes being true to your beliefs. It will improve your business and your relationships, too.

Pay yourself first—meaning save your money by depositing a regular dollar amount every paycheck. I realize that money is not the root of all evil, but is a way to support your family and yourself as well as contribute to charity and retirement.

If a woman wishes to connect with me, this way is best —
Karendeis.com

THIRTY-SIX

SUE MCKINNEY

God gave us two ears, and one mouth. Use them in that order. Don't be so quick to be 'right'; listen first.

What would I say to my younger self?

1. Don't be afraid to take risks.
2. Listen to your Mother. No matter how much you dislike her, she will always be your best friend.
3. That 17-year-old boy does NOT love you. He just wants into your pants.
4. Don't argue with people, waste of time.
5. Be yourself. It's enough.

If a woman wishes to connect with me, this way is best —
https://www.facebook.com/sue.mckinney.142

THIRTY-SEVEN

SHELLIE HIPSKY

My secret to being wiser can be witnessed in my life-long connections with other powerful and intelligent women. When I was able to do a true self-assessment of my strengths and needs, I identified how I could best contribute to others and their missions; because of this, I can count on them to fill in my gaps of understanding and resources. The women in my Global Sisterhood ™ lift each other up and lend their skills and talents so that we can build on each other's foundations.

Yes, I have book smarts as evidenced by the decade of teaching I did at the Ph.D. level in the Global Perspective as a tenured professor and the books I have authored that went on to become International Best Sellers such as my Common Threads trilogy. Yet, it if wasn't for the brilliance of the top 100 women who I interviewed for the books on Inspiration, Empowerment, and Balance for Empowering Women Radio and Common Threads, I would not be as wise on a deeper level about the various vital topics.

Now my non-profit charity, the Global Sisterhood harnesses the power of these friendships and helps women and girls around the world by providing resources and networks to make dreams and goals a reality.

What would I say to my younger self?

Dear Young Me,

You can manifest your dream life. Enjoy the journey. Steer clear of overly "charming" men. You are worthy of so much more than you know.

Give back to others and then do it some more. It is through your volunteering and love that you will change the world. Speaking of that, there will be nay-sayers who don't get your vision; however, there will come a time when the important people will embrace it on an international level.

Until then, be you—authentically, over-the-top you!

Love,

40 and Wiser Me

If a woman wishes to connect with me, this way is best —
www.InspiringLivesInternational.com
www.GlobalSisterhoodOnline.org

THIRTY-EIGHT

CARYN CHOW

I f any woman came to me asked for my number one inside secret to being wiser, I would say, don't believe everything you tell yourself.

What I would say to my younger self is that your journey will be like the ocean with tides high and low, waves gentle and rough.

Trust the process because in the end there will be smooth sailing and an outcome well worth waiting for.

If a woman wishes to connect with me, this way is best —
https://www.facebook.com/Caryn.A.Chow

THIRTY-NINE

KIM SWANEY

My number one wisdom secret is to not follow those that don't have what you want.

Find a mentor and follow those who have done what you want to do!

Strive to always be of service to others and don't sweat the small stuff.

READ, READ, READ!

That is all we need!

If a woman wishes to connect with me, this way is best — https://www.facebook.com/happinessthroughhorses

FORTY

DOLORES SHEETS

believe the number one secret of being wiser is listening to others and being engaged and present in the conversation.

What I would say to my younger self is to never give up on your dreams. Work toward your goals every day.

If a woman wishes to connect with me, this way is best —
http://www.sheetstaxes.com/

FORTY-ONE

Cal

"Hello, it's me. Hello, it's me. I was wondering if after all these years you'd like to meet. To go over everything. They say that time's supposed to heal ya, but I ain't done much healing...

Hello, can you hear me? I'm in California dreaming about who we used to be when we were younger and free. I've forgotten how it felt before the world fell at our feet. There's such a difference between us, and a million miles...

Hello from the other side..."

Adelle, of course, was looking back at a lost love in her song. When I read Jessica's questions, I imagined Adelle's lost love as a younger, more innocent me. And I wondered. What might the conversation be between me now and me as a younger self at some pivotal point in our life?

Am I in fact wiser now? Is so, what sage advice would I give that perhaps should have been considered as I approached an important fork along my path into the future?

That pivotal juncture for me came as early as the summer between my Junior and Senior years of high school—the summer I met my husband to be. My advice? Love him. You will have happy times. Don't build the house on the mountain, you will cry when you sell it and cry again when it burns down. And most important, do not buy into his self-defeating, and ego shattering words.

Listen to your Mother. The beliefs she taught you, these truths, are yours to embrace—stick to them:

You are worthy.

You are smart.

You are strong.

You are more beautiful inside than out.

You are more than he wants you to believe possible.

And most of all, you are all of this and more with or without him—it's your choice to make.

The secret to being wiser is clarity. Becoming clear about what you want and who you are at any given moment in time exposes a broad vista of opportunities from which you can choose; any one of which will lead to who will you be tomorrow and the next day and the next.

Never stop learning, growing as a person, and evolving. Surround yourself with like-minded people. As Steve Harvey said, "Stop telling your big dreams to small minded people."

If a woman wishes to connect with me, this way is best —
http://www.writingbytes.com
https://www.facebook.com/czscribe

KAY WATSON

Make sure you understand the power of limiting beliefs and check yourself every day to be sure you are overcoming them.

Learn to ignore everything that does not ring true with your heart.

If a woman wishes to connect with me, this way is best —
Kay@pkeastman.com

PAULA LEMLEY MILES

Hone your listening skills. First step is to listen to what God is speaking to you. It is only by listening clearly to Him, can you properly listen to others.

When someone is speaking to you in an interpersonal exchange, value the interaction. Hear what they are saying and what they are NOT saying.

Don't be in a hurry to share your thoughts until they have completed their thoughts. If you jump ahead based off of one component of their conversation, you may entirely miss the most vital information. Don't be planning dinner or making a mental grocery list or any other diversion.

Focus on what they are saying in the moment. Genuine listening conveys more about how much you care than any other skill.

Don't become hurt or angry if people don't respond or act in a situation as I would if the circumstances were reversed. Everyone has different gifts and talents.

Expecting others to be mind readers about my needs or wants is not fair. The lack of a response as I would give is not an indicator of that person's level of caring for me.

If a woman wishes to connect with me, this way is best — https://www.facebook.com/pjmpoet

FORTY-FOUR

RACHEL RAKOVAN

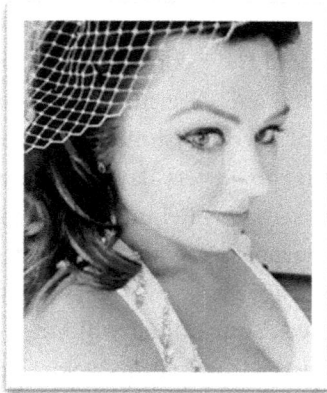

The most vital piece of advice that I can provide is to not expect anything from anyone. When we have attachments that transfer our responsibilities or validation onto others, that takes our power and we are left wondering whether the task that needs fulfilled will be completed; or if what we have done, or the way we look, is enough. We wonder if we meet someone else's standard of attraction or if our assets are considered wealthy—in their perspective. We open ourselves to vulnerability and allow others to control our destiny by attaching our self-worth or future accomplishments to their whim. When we take full responsibility for ourselves and our future, this is when we are truly free. When we sever attachments that make us rely on others for validation, enhancements, or even friendship, we relieve ourselves of suffering.

Removing expectation from our lives and knowing that nothing will be accomplished unless we do everything ourselves, motivates us to become our best selves.

Do your best always and do it for yourself and to help others. Regret is no way to live and placing blame on others for not helping you or validating you is a direct path to unhappiness. No one will make you their number one priority above themselves. That's your job! Have confidence and believe in yourself always. Pace your life and determine what is most important. Strategize a plan of accomplishment by creating a goal and working toward that goal every day in some way.

To my younger self, I say helping others and being a servant is everyone's life purpose. We are all chosen to help others in some way. We may not yet know the path, but we must listen to our internal voice. Your calling will not come from an outside source; it will come from within in you. You will burst with emotion and in your soul you will know your life's purpose. The best way to find that purpose is through reading and talking to other people about their career paths.

Some do not know their life's purpose because they have many talents and passions. Our paths are like a garden that only has so much water; we choose one or two flowers to water, otherwise none of these talents will grow. Water most the talents or careers that you choose and you will have expertise that will truly help others. Your other talents can be pursued as hobbies to reinforce your passions. You may find a way to combine passions in an entrepreneurial fashion. However, if it is not a passion that helps others, it is likely not the passion to be pursued.

If a woman wishes to connect with me, this way is best —
https://www.facebook.com/rachel.rakovan

FORTY-FIVE

CARMELIA RAY

My number one secret to being wiser is to not fear making mistakes or having the regret of NOT taking action when opportunity knocks.

I have made many mistakes growing up in the dating and matchmaking business by biting off more than I could chew. Some may not agree with this practice but I discovered by taking risks and putting myself out there in situations that I was not comfortable with, it allowed me to gain experience and learn from my mistakes and failures.

If there's something you don't know, figure it out! Seek people who can help you. Find a mentor. Do your homework. Do your research. Be hungry for knowledge and never stop asking questions until you find your answer. There may be many answers to the same question.

Perspective is everything.

I would say to my younger self, be motivated by self-love and respect. In all your choices consider the impact of your decisions to you physically, emotionally, and mentally.

I would tell myself to consider the big picture and to exercise patience. In many cases you are better off waiting for the right opportunity, being selective instead of taking on everything that comes your way. Don't be concerned with FOMO "fear of missing out" if it doesn't truly inspire you.

I would tell my younger self not to get caught up with the stories my negative inside voice tells me when it whispers, you can't do it, you're not good enough or you will make a fool of yourself. Ignore messages and feelings of doubt and replace them with feelings of hope, love and acceptance.

Be graceful. Be grateful and always tell your parents you love them no matter what.

If a woman wishes to connect with me, this way is best —
www.carmeliaray.com

FORTY-SIX

LARONDA ROBINSON

I f any woman came to me and asked for my number one insider secret to being wiser, I would let her know that every person she meets has something to teach her. I would tell her to give everyone the love, respect, and consideration that she wants for herself.

What would I say to my younger self? LaRonda, where you started isn't half as important as where you choose to go. You are worthy of love. Never settle for less than you deserve. It's OK to play as hard as you work.

If a woman wishes to connect with me, this way is best —
Larondarobinson@live.com

FORTY-SEVEN

SHILEEN NIXON

As I think about my answer to the questions about my number one secret to being wiser and what I would say to my younger self, I can't help but think of my grown boys (ages 23 and 28).

They are doing such amazing things with their lives as they both are operating from a place of authenticity and tapping into and developing their life passions.

When I express my amazement with what all they do and how much they truly inspire me, they always say to me, "Mom, we are just doing what you taught us to do!" and they proceed to thank me. It's humbling to say the least as well as gratifying as a mother, especially knowing that as they were growing up, life was less than perfect! So, my answer lies within the framework of my grown boys.

Embrace the essence of who you are and celebrate the magnificent creation that you are. There is only one you! There is no one else in this universe who can be you in any way shape or form nor do what you do the way you can do it.

What is held within you as you can only be expressed by you, and that expression has your one and only unique thumbprint imprinted on and through what you create in life. What you express and create authentically as you, and with you being so very precious, makes all that you are and all that you express in life so beautiful and precious as well!

Therefore, live your life fearlessly and lovingly! Be yourself fearlessly and outrageously! Tap into what makes you tick by playfully discover what makes your heart sing. Take those discoveries and create your dreams. You can do anything you set your mind to do, so order your steps in life in a way that match your dreams.

And remember, love is the greatest healer of all. Living authentically is living from a place of love and that is where life and momentum is given to your dreams. As you continue to embrace your beautiful essence and live authentically, you will wake up one day to find that your dreams have become your way of life.

If a woman wishes to connect with me, this way is best —
shileennixon@gmail.com

FORTY-EIGHT

DR. WANG

Be true to yourself. Know your strengths and weaknesses.

Set a goal and work hard to achieve it. However, if it doesn't work out, be flexible to change.

Often a door closes and a window opens elsewhere. Enjoy and have fun. You can't be serious all the time.

Be sweet, kind, and generous, Smile often and sincerely.

Keep in touch with family and friends.

Work hard but also cultivate a passion or hobby.

Maintain balance. Strive for good health. Embrace serenity within ourselves and peace around us.

If a woman wishes to connect with me, this way is best —
https://www.facebook.com/HolisticHealer81

FORTY-NINE

TANYA WILLIAMS

Wisdom comes from understanding the circumstances of a particular issue therefore it is imperative to listen far more than you speak.

Most importantly, make all important decisions after meditation, prayer, and a response from your gut!

What would I say to my younger self?

Tanya, relax, have more fun. No one expects you always be the good girl.

If a woman wishes to connect with me, this way is best —
@Imtanyawilliams – Twitter

FIFTY

MIA VOSS

would tell my younger self to be my own best friend. It creates a solid sense of self and you end up using your judgement much more and not doubting yourself.

I've found the best way to connect with anyone is by genuinely complimenting them! Anything: shoes, social posts, smarts.

Practical advice to my younger self: moisturize and wear sunblock!!

If a woman wishes to connect with me, this way is best —
Miaonthego.com

FIFTY-ONE

SALLY HENDRICK

Not every opportunity is something you should take. Stay focused on what you should be doing with your life. Keep a list of everything that you want in life regarding family, career, health, and something else random that's important to you.

Consider decisions that take up your time and energy with careful thought. If opportunities that arise do not serve your vision, move on.

Learn to say no tactfully, diplomatically, and with grace.

You do not have to be super woman. I'm still battling that.

If a woman wishes to connect with me, this way is best —
50ShadesOfOrangeClub.com

FIFTY-TWO

DR. CORTNEY BAKER

*S*tay true to your internal moral compass. And in a world full of rhinestones, be a diamond.

I had my son at 19 and so I would mainly tell my younger self to trust God and to know that He will never let her down.

If a woman wishes to connect with me, this way is best —
https://www.facebook.com/cortneyabaker

FIFTY-THREE

STACY JOHNSON

would tell young Stacy that she is enough and not to doubt that. The universe loves you, and don't undervalue yourself. I would say that if she saw what I see when I look at her then she would believe. Sometimes you'll be too much woman, too smart, too beautiful, too strong, too much of something that makes a man feel like less of a man, which will start making you feel like you have to be less of a woman. The biggest mistake you can make is to remove jewels from your crown to make it easier for a man to carry. When this happens, I need you to understand, you do not need a smaller crown—you need a man with bigger hands.

Oh and that guy in Pennington's writing class? He's the one.

If a woman wishes to connect with me, this way is best —
https://www.facebook.com/stacyj9

FIFTY-FOUR

MARTIÑA REYES

o you remember what you wanted to be, as a child, when you grew up? Are you doing what you dreamed? Has your dream become your reality?

When I was young, I was fascinated by nature. Actually, I still am. As a Caribbean girl, I lived in the enchanted Island of Puerto Rico. Here I spent hours laying in the sand feeling the breeze of the Caribbean Sea with the warm sun in my face. Looking up into the clouds I imagined animals, fruits and all sort of shapes, colors, and sometimes even how it all smelled. In my mind it became so vivid that I felt with all my senses as if it all was real.

As we get older we keep imagining, but sometimes dreams and desires start to fade away. I often wonder why is it that when we grow up, we forget those things that we dreamed of becoming and become what society tells us we should be?

As we grow up, we women tend to prioritize our family, our home, business, and the day to day chores; sometimes dealing with unexpected obstacles not planned or pursued. It is often a challenge to make time for ourselves.

The difference is that those who don't use their imagination beyond the beliefs that they grew up with will repeat the same learned behavior around them and won't evolve into the women they were born to be. Those who dare to imagine beyond that set of beliefs discover that some beliefs are no longer useful, and that they can create new and powerful habits that eventually help them achieve greatness in their lives.

The key is simple: Choose to adopt a daring imagination and your mind and actions will adjust. This will become part of your personality and help create the person you deserve to be.

I remember in junior high school my dancing teacher, one of my first mentors, telling me to visualize myself not only performing at my greatest, but wining a dance competition. Years later I won several of them. As I envisioned the steps, I rehearsed and developed confidence in my mind. Since that time I have taken her words and lived my life through them. I promised myself to always imagine what I want to create in my life.

When you keep picturing long enough and practicing whatever you want to achieve, pretty soon you'll forget that you are imagining. One day you will find that you are doing it for real with a lot of success. The more empowering your imagination is, the better your life will be.

Take a moment and close your eyes. Imagine and feel the joy and excitement of witnessing, through your imagination, your personal transformation. Now celebrate what you have accomplished in your mind. Right at this moment I am pretty sure you have a big smile in your gorgeous face. This is because your mind is connected to your body.

Every night, before falling asleep, I experience the same feeling of joy and excitement you just felt. I imagine waking up the next morning in gratitude ready to meet someone who could teach me something new. It could be face to face, through the Internet or from a powerful book that will help me reach my next mile-stone, one day at a time. I assure you this exercise will take only a couple of minutes every night and will do wonders in your life.

Remember when you were a child and played imagining those things you loved back then? Like I did, drawing the clouds in the sky? Everything is possible in an innocent imagination, that's the one you must activate. If I could tell my younger self one thing it would be: Never stop imagining!

Be a true believer, keep working the right way, trying new ideas and trust your intuition. Whatever you create with love and passion in your imagination, one day may come true.

Dare to Imagine has been the mantra, the attitude that has shaped the woman I am today and the one I shall become tomorrow. Today I pass on the secret to you. This is the most powerful step to reprogram your mindset for success. If you can imagine, you can be-come anything you want and a bit more. Every time you hear that little voice telling you If Only..., Dare to Imagine and that little voice will go away.

> *If a woman wishes to connect with me, this way is best —*
> martina@martinareyes.com

FIFTY-FIVE

SABRINA RISLEY

Be authentic. People want to get to know you, the real you. Take a chance.

Be authentic to who you are and try not to worry what others think or how they may judge you. Those who are meant to be in your life will always be there and those who aren't will filter themselves out. Distill your life down to those who love and accept you for who you are.

In a world that's constantly trying to make us someone we're not, just be yourself.

If a woman wishes to connect with me, this way is best —
https://www.facebook.com/sabrinarisley

FIFTY-SIX

JAN VERHOEFF

My number one secret is relying on the Bible; the answers really are in the pages of the Bible. Although I continue learning all the time, and use any resources available, I find I prove the lessons by looking back to the Bible to make sure they're true and real. On those occasions when I find a lesson isn't truth, I leave it behind, and keep learning.

Always look for the best life offers, and learn from life, but hold tight to the promises and learn to let go of the problems.

Solutions come with action, so I've learned to take action on solving problems and know that I'm going the right direction.

Faith is the victory—and I know my faith in Christ is the basis of all wisdom.

Never stop giving, even though you know sometimes the outcome isn't going to be good. Never give up. And never stop giving more of yourself, more of what you have, and more of God's blessings to others. You can't out give God and He is your provider. Trust and keep giving. Ask with expectation. God provides abundantly, all you have to do is ask and he will provide the desires of your heart.

ALWAYS be grateful. The key is to give first, ask after, and be grateful.

If a woman wishes to connect with me, this way is best — www.JanVerhoeff.com

FIFTY-SEVEN

GINA CARR

Forgive quickly. Unforgiven transgressions are not worth the pain that comes from a lost relationship and harbored anger.

Find that thing that really makes your heart sing and pursue it with all the passion you can muster. If you focus, you will figure out how to make a great living doing what really makes you happy.

If a woman wishes to connect with me, this way is best —
https://www.facebook.com/GinaCarr

FIFTY-EIGHT

MICHELLE HOLDERNESS

Believe in myself and my God given ability.

Quit thinking that everyone else is better and smarter.

If a woman wishes to connect with me, this way is best —

FIFTY-NINE

DEBBIE LINDT

Don't let fear stop you for becoming all you were created to be. Do away with fear of not being liked, fear of making the wrong decision, fear of doing it wrong. Be fearless!!

If a woman wishes to connect with me, this way is best — https://www.facebook.com/debbie.lindt

KAREN GOOSEN MONTOYA

A lways be kind to yourself.
We are so hard on ourselves.
Everything always has a way of working out.
No need to worry so much.

If a woman wishes to connect with me, this way is best —
Shiftojoy.com

YVONNE A. JONES

Be decisive, yet selective. Do not be afraid to be different in your opinions and views. You do not have to be one of the pack. People may initially think you're odd, but once they get to know you and come to recognize that there is strength and confidence in what you stand for, they come to respect and appreciate you. It's called Standing in your Power.

Be authentic.

Be kind.

Be others-focused.

Love yourself so that you can love others.

Do not compromise your values and standards for anyone. You have to live with your conscience.

To my younger self I say, even though you may be surrounded by good influences and influencers, take the time to get to know yourself, identify who and what YOU want in your life so that you make the best possible choices, and always with God's guidance. You have to live with your choices, no one else.

Don't be in a hurry to make decisions out of fear that opportunities may not be open to you again. They always are, and the best ones often take longer to appear.

If a woman wishes to connect with me, this way is best —
yvonne@yvonneajones.com

SIXTY-TWO

ELLEN SHAYMAN ROGIN

To be great with money save at least 10%, give away at least 10%, and picture your prosperity.

The best way to be happy and successful is to give what you most desire.

If a woman wishes to connect with me, this way is best —
https://www.facebook.com/ellenrogin

SIXTY-THREE

VERONICA KOLIBAB

Know your value. I believe most unhealthy decisions in our lives stem from a belief that we are not worthy. It is programming from birth through experiences in life, all valuable of course, that bring us to where we stand in this moment.

Each of us are unique and spectacular. We all have gifts and talents that we bring into this life.

Once I learned my value, my whole world shifted and as I honored me, my whole world did as well.

If a woman wishes to connect with me, this way is best —
https://www.facebook.com/veronicakolibab

SIXTY-FOUR

JENNIFER TAPSCOTT

ife should be lived without regrets. Everything teaches us something.

Hang in there because life will only get better with age.

You got this!

If a woman wishes to connect with me, this way is best —
https://www.facebook.com/babyblackbirds

SIXTY-FIVE

RACHEL MARTIN

D o not forget yourself in your life journey. Sometimes life, or motherhood, can take all the time and the dreams that we have can be put on hold.

I'd say, don't do anything to put those dreams on hold, but to constantly be fighting for your heart and dreams.

If a woman wishes to connect with me, this way is best —
Findingjoy.net

SIXTY-SIX

WENDI HATTON

My biggest secret is knowing what your passion is and going for it. Find people who are where you want to be, take their advice seriously, and implement! I would say to my younger self, dream big! Find your path to success and pour yourself into learning every detail around your vision. You might not know exactly how to get there, but as long as you know what the end result is, keep your eye on it and you will get there. You have the power to become or do anything you want in life. Just decide, and get started on your journey and you will absolutely have more success than you could ever imagine!

If a woman wishes to connect with me, this way is best —
wendi@wendihatton.com

SIXTY-SEVEN

JERRILYN B THOMAS

Understanding that I am only human NOT superhuman. I use my personal and business failures as stepping stones to create something better. I give myself a short period to wallow in woe is me, then I shake it off and take inventory to see what worked and what didn't work.

I take what worked and use it as part of my reinvention. Life isn't static. You have to continually shed your skin to expand your knowledge.

Learn to relax and smell the flowers. Put yourself first. Have more courage and faith in yourself. Invest, invest, invest to ensure you have a safety net.

If a woman wishes to connect with me, this way is best —
jerrilynnbthomas@gmail.com

141

SIXTY-EIGHT

HOPE H. ANDERSON

would boldly tell her to know that we are all complete from the moment we enter the world and that we can become anything we want to become when we know that we are in charge of our purposeful intentions. We will come to know that we are in charge of our world.

Allow God to speak to us through the way we treat each other with respect, giving empathy, loving one another, and in making peace through our actions. That is what we all have to give away in making this world a better place for all.

I would say to my younger self that all the changes I experienced were necessary, as difficult and unbearable that life seemed sometimes as I look back.

But now, I realize that they were all necessary because they form my character and mold me into the person I am today.

I am thoughtful, kind, and have a purpose to make a difference in the world as a force for good in living and giving. Those experiences became a reality and allowed me the wisdom to be grateful for living an abundant life filled with joy and happiness.

This mantra reminds me of what is important: Never give up, believe in myself, and push forward No Matter What!

If a woman wishes to connect with me, this way is best —
Hopenutriservices.com

SUMMER WHITSELL HANKINS

K now yourself. Every mistake you make makes you wiser and is a lesson so move forward, because we aren't perfect.

If a woman wishes to connect with me, this way is best — https://www.facebook.com/summer.whitsellhankins

VICKY MCLEOD

O ur ability to hold both strength and vulnerability is a power that is changing the world. Whatever it is you want for yourself, your children, or the planet, be that thing and the gods will dance to your tune.

We're not in this alone. Reach out to other women. Support them. Love them. And let them love and support you back. We make our most beautiful music together.

Fall completely in love with yourself. It is the most interesting relationship you will ever have, and from that one loving relationship all things will be possible.

If you have the choice between shallow or deep, pick deep. It's more challenging but also more fun. It is also where you will discover the magic.

Love what you love.

Unabashedly.

Enthusiastically.

Passionately.

The world needs more passion. Specifically, it needs yours. Don't hold back or hold out. Give everything. Kiss with your mouth open.

Never be afraid to take your own side.

If a woman wishes to connect with me, this way is best — vickimcleod.com

About the Authors
Yvonne A. Jones

Yvonne A Jones is your Customer Relationship Specialist and Online Marketing Strategist. She is a Certified International Speaker, Business Coach and Mentor who supports businesses and highly-motivated entrepreneurs on how to use Online Marketing and Social Media Marketing to attract customers, and how to retain them by using Customer Relationship Marketing strategies so they become loyal customers and raving fans.

Yvonne helps you to bring your offline business online and create a nurturing environment for your clients and customers.

Yvonne spent over 35 years in Banking, Human Resources and Administration, and combines that experience with owning three businesses, including an "S" Corporation which provided Inbound Callers with one-time resolution, before moving to Online Marketing in 2008. She's an avid Blogger

who has written over 400 articles and blog posts, multiple e-books, and published on Kindle.

She is a Founding and Lifetime Member of Women's Prosperity Network, and Co-Chapter Leader of the Jamaica Chapter.

She was listed on HuffingtonPost.com as one of the "Top 100 Most Social Customer Service Pros on Twitter." And on LinkedIn as one of the "Top 100 Women to Connect with on LinkedIn."

Yvonne returned to live in Jamaica in 2015 after spending 26 years in the United States.

She is married with three daughters, three sons-in-law, and 3 delightful grand-children.

Her burning desire is to empower others to succeed on their own terms and bring transformation to their own lives so they uncover any blocks in their life and business.

If a woman wishes to connect with me, this way is best —

http://YvonneAJones.com

http://ArticlesbyYvonneAJones.com

https://jm.linkedin.com/in/yvonneajones

http://Twitter.com/YvonneAJones

https://Facebook.com/YvonneAJones

http://Facebook.com/SocialMediaandCustomerService

http://Pinterest.com/YvonneAJones

About the Authors
Jessica Peterson

After a 20-year career in the banking and financial world, Jessica desired to create an agency that had a positive impact for businesses and for their clients. Over her 20-year career, she was top sales consistently while creating and implementing strategy using social media. She is passionate in volunteering, reading, traveling, speaking. Everyone knows Jessica as a Connector and Supporter and now as a multi-published author.

Jessica has been married for 18 years to Evan and they have a daughter who truly is a blessing after having been advised they could not have children. They both learned to never say never!

In 2016, Jessica launched Knot Brothers, one of her dreams. The international men's clothing line, in its first 30 days, garnered 100,000 orders through social media connections!

Jessica has won many awards including: top sales, top employee, and top 12 Spirited Women, as well as being featured as a Top 100 Empowering Woman in the International Best Selling book, *Common Threads* by Dr. Shellie Hipsky. In 2016 she had the honor of being a TEDx speaker in Colorado.

After years of experience and testing social media, Jessica developed a 4-step plan of action to grow your business on social media. With this 4-Step Success Plan, she has grown an affiliate team of over 3,000 sales associates worldwide in one year and was selected as top speaker and trainer out of 260,000 people.

She has coached social media experts and worked with clients around the world. Her clients include:

Celebrities

Mortgage professionals

Insurance agents

Coaches

Speakers

New developments and communities

Sales professionals

Social media experts

International and national real estate, including resorts and islands.

A letter from Jessica's heart

As I write this letter, I am filled with gratitude for all of the blessings that I have received from my clients, friends, and associates who have been part of my business growth and achievement with Customer-WowPro-ject.com. I am often asked to share "the secret" to my success and I felt I could do that best by giving you a bit more information about me personally and how I came to be where I am today.

Twenty years ago, I began a career in the banking industry. It was a great opportunity for me and I was honored to be recognized as a top sales performer during my very first year. The thank you cards (and gifts) started pouring in! It felt wonderful to be appreciated for taking care of the clients. As my career progressed, I continued to be awarded as employee of the month and top sales leader many times. And how did I do this? Well, the secret to this success is that I genuinely cared about each and every person with whom I came into contact and worked very hard to achieve the best possible outcome for them.

It is no surprise to learn the Journal of Socio-Economics states that your relationships are worth more than $100,000. In one compelling study, a key difference between very happy people and less-happy people was good relationships. Happier people also live longer and show significantly lower blood pressure—good news all the way around.

Over time, I started to recognize the incredible power of social media and its ability to connect people and offer them an efficient way to stay connected and stay in touch with people.

When Facebook was launched (and after much re-search and study), I began using it and it was amazing how quickly I was able to generate even more business through proper use of the platform. I also began using Twitter with the same results—increased business—just by staying in touch with my customers. I knew that I had the ability to help others achieve the same results, which led me to create a program that assists people in using all social media channels to increase their businesses.

Connecting through social media and offline are both important ways to show people that you run a business that genuinely cares about its customers. Consider this powerful information:

> 74% of consumers identify word of mouth marketing as a key influencer in their purchasing decision. (Ogilvy / Google / TNS)

> Brands that inspire a higher emotional intensity receive three times as much word of mouth marketing as less emotionally connected brands. (Keller Fay Group)

And while statistics are important, real life examples really bring forth the benefit to you and your business. One of our clients is Steve who is an insurance broker. Fifteen days after implementing our personalized social media Facebook coaching system, he generated over $32,000 in revenue. He discovered the power of influence and word of mouth marketing with Facebook. Even better, he is enjoying his new business relationships and the enrichment that they bring to his life.

Looking back, when I left the banking industry, my plan was to retire. I wanted to volunteer in my community and spend more time with my husband and daughter. But the overwhelming need to help others grow their business by reaching out (and taking care of their clients) wouldn't go away. I knew for a fact that many business owners were frantically chasing the next deal, losing touch with their former clients, and leaving those clients feeling under-appreciated. To me this just did not make sense on either a financial or customer service level. I had to share this with people, and once I did, I started to generate business for a company (customer-wowproject.com) that did not even exist yet!

I officially began in March of 2012 and since then have continued to grow my business (and those of my clients) by creating a toolkit of online and offline pro-grams that build business relationships and increase the most valuable type of advertising of all, word of mouth marketing.

This led to the creation of my certification program that guides people through the steps of creating dialog with their client base to become a WOW Giver—someone who has taken our training to build business relationships with a specific goal: growth while making a positive impact on those that they serve. This training teaches how to use Facebook to grow your business and apply the learned principles in other areas of your business, including other social media channels. It brings me joy when people share with me how they are able to expand on the training and use what they learned in other social media channels with success.

A company that completes our training is given a WOW Giver certificate. WOW Givers are dedicated to the following principles:

- We have an honest and sincere desire to support businesses and individuals in the communities we serve
- We want to assist other businesses in meeting their growth objectives
- We genuinely care—and stay in touch through Facebook, other social media outlets and tele-phone and in-person contact
- WOW Givers connect people in their community and around the world to the right resources to fulfill their dreams and goals
- We strive to make a positive impact in everything we do.

JESSICA'S BOOKS

AUTHORED BOOKS

WOW on Facebook
WOW Now Increase Revenue
(book gifted at customerwowproject.com)

FEATURED IN

Common Threads Balance
Market Me

New Book! ARRIVING IN 2016

Purpose Powered People

A GIFT FOR YOU

Thank you for taking the time to download and read this book. We have a gift waiting for you on the Customer WOW Project's website: www.customerwowproject.com

Grab it now for free: 100k Social Media Blueprint!

Bonus: Your 30-day Wow Now Success Kit

From Our Readers...

"After reading only the first few chapters, I realized that this book is simply about life. It's for everyone—man, woman, and child—to read. This gift of wisdom is what I wish someone had shared with me when I was a young man.

Parents need to hand this book to their children and make sure they read it. I want my daughter to read it and to know that what the women in this book have to say is the wisdom I would gift her with, if I had the words." —*Robert Droysen*

"Inspiring! Uplifting! A great tool to motivate my spirit, even when I'm feeling confident.

When I stay connected with people who are confident then I can remain in that place longer which is a big mission in my life." —*Michelle Trimarco*

"This book brought much needed joy to my heart. Every day is a new day, because tomorrow may never come. Don't wait. This book is a must read to get you through bumps in life and avoid them. For a while I had a dormant life and this pushed me through. It made feel ok about life and inspired." —*Martha Hill*

"This book empowers young women today to live a wiser life and make choices that lead to happiness. In truth, the advice Jessica and Yvonne garnered from 70 amazing women enriches the lives of all who take heed. I am honored to publish a book as filled with purpose and wisdom as this, and am wiser myself for having played a part in this grand mission to make a difference in people's lives". —*Candy Zulkosky, Founder BytesPress Publishing*

"Peterson's book is a fascinating tour through a range of various significant women's lives, and nicely intertwines the common theme of what it takes to be a successful woman today. I found this book to be an anthology of intelligence, motivation, and encouragement in the race of succeeding as a woman in today's often discouraging world.

Whatever your mission in life, this is a feel good collection of experiences that will surly motivate you to examine the way you think about your approach in succeeding, big or small.

What a unique and creative way for an author to create a book that serves as a tool to inspire and lead!" —*Melissa Whitmore*

www.ingramcontent.com/pod-product-compliance
Lightning Source LLC
Chambersburg PA
CBHW072012290326
41934CB00007BA/1061